OUR WORLD IN COLOUR
THE GOLDEN TEMPLE

OUR WORLD IN COLOUR
THE GOLDEN TEMPLE

Photography by Sondeep Shankar
Text by Dr Mohinder Singh

(half title page)
A golden panel from the doors of the temple depicting the third Guru, Amar Dass, with his disciples.

(title spread)
The Golden Temple or Harmandir Sahib is situated in the centre of a tank or sarovar. *The Darshani Deohri is the gateway from which the causeway leads to the temple.*

(page 5)
Guru Nanak reconciled Hindu and Muslim traditions to establish the Sikh faith, one of the youngest of world religions. He is often fondly known as the 'Guru of the Hindus and Pir of the Muslims'. In this mural painting Guru Nanak is shown with his companions Mardana, a Muslim rabab *player and Bala, a Hindu who accompanied him on his journeys.*

(pages 6-7)
A view of the main entrance known as Ghantaghar. Beneath the clock tower is the information office and shops selling Sikh literature and souvenirs.

(pages 8-9)
The golden plaques on the doors of the main temple were presented by Maharaja Ranjit Singh who ruled the Punjab from 1799 to 1838. The doors are divided into several sections; each plate is made of beaten gold and depicts scenes from the lives of the gurus. These plates are now preserved in the temple treasury but are displayed during certain festivals.

(pages 10-11)
Young children dressed as Panj Piaras, 'the Five Beloved Ones', heroes of the Sikh tradition.

Text and captions by Dr Mohinder Singh
Photography by Sondeep Shankar
Additional photography supplied courtesy of Toby Sinclair for page 13

The author and publisher would like to thank the Secretary of the SGPC Amritsar for his help and advice.

Editor: May Holdsworth
Series Editor: Caroline Robertson
Designers: David Hurst and Teresa Ho
Created by Gulmohur Press

Production House: Twin Age Ltd, Hong Kong

Printed in China

ISBN 962-217-167-2

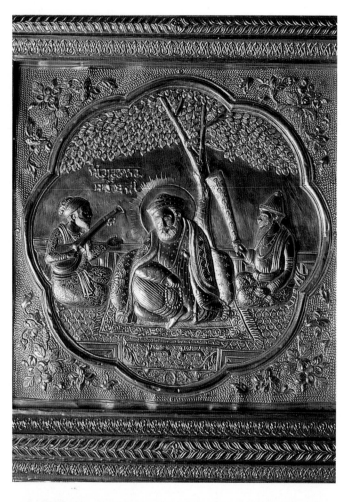

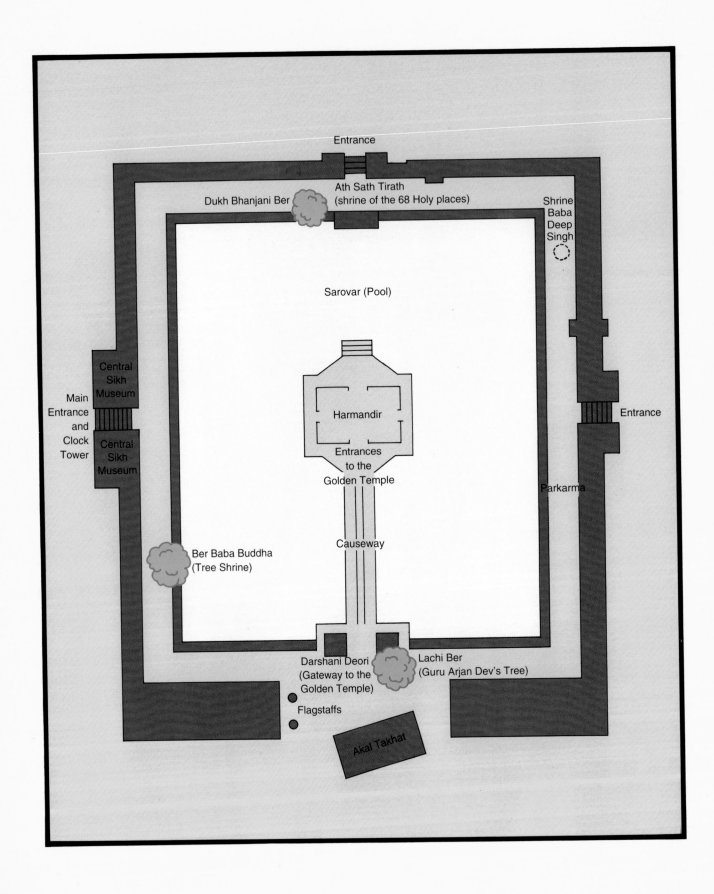

D ISTINGUISHED BY THEIR TYPICAL TURBANS AND UNTRIMMED HAIR, VIGOUR and enterprising spirit, the Sikhs are a virile and colourful people. Though mainly concentrated in the Indian state of Punjab after the partition of the sub-continent in 1947, they are settled in almost all parts of India as well as in many countries abroad. The Sikhs have done well for themselves in India, and made a major contribution to her agriculture and defence, while in foreign lands they have proved to be an adventurous and hard-working migrant group. While they have a tremendous capacity to confront challenging situations, what chiefly distinguishes them as a community is the tenacity of their cultural and religious heritage.

The term 'Sikh', derived from the Sanskrit word *shishya* meaning disciple or learner, was used for the followers of Guru Nanak, the founder of the Sikh faith. There were ten gurus beginning with Nanak and ending with Gobind Singh, who died in 1708. Reverence for the gurus and devotion to their teachings was a cardinal principle of this faith. Another aspect of the religion is its great emphasis on integrating moral and spiritual values into everyday life.

A reproduction of a painting of Maharaja Ranjit Singh done by G T Vigne in 1837. Ranjit Singh was responsible for renovating the Golden Temple and many of his priceless gifts are preserved in the temple treasury.

THE FOUNDER AND HIS TEACHINGS

Guru Nanak (1469–1539) possessed a deeply meditative cast of mind from childhood and showed little interest in worldly pursuits, preferring to serve the poor and needy. After his marriage Nanak was sent to Sultanpur Lodhi where he was employed as store-keeper of the local ruler. It was during this period, according to popular belief, that Nanak received his Enlightenment: one morning, bathing in the river Bein nearby, he entered deep into meditation and was admitted to the Divine Presence. Blessed by the Almighty, Nanak emerged from the river to preach the Holy Name. The first words that he uttered, expressing his new mission of reconciliation, were 'There is no Hindu, there is no Musalman.' Accompanied by a Muslim musician named Mardana and a Hindu named Bala, the Guru set out to preach his gospel of love and truth. He travelled long distances to different parts of India and neighbouring countries, visiting religious centres of both Hindus and Muslims. Through dialogue he convinced people that good actions alone could ensure salvation. While in Mecca he was asked who was superior, a Hindu or a Muslim, to which the Guru replied that without virtue in action neither was of any consequence.

Guru Nanak preached monotheism and described the Creator as *Ikk* (One), without a second. His philosophy is best set forth in *Japji*, the primary creed. In contrast to the medieval Indian practice of renouncing the world for spiritual elevation, Nanak taught that spirituality was a component of everyday life.

Guru Nanak's teachings can be summed up in three simple Punjabi injunctions; *naam japna, kirt karni and wand chakhna*—hold God in your heart, live by honest means and share the fruits of your labour. Guru Nanak started the twin institutions of *Sangat* (congregation) and *Pangat* (commensality), emphasising community participation and the sharing of resources: all would sit on the floor without distinction of status or wealth and eat together without differentiation of caste. This was for its time a revolutionary credo.

(top) *Pilgrims from near and far travel to Amritsar throughout the year to pay respects at the holiest of Sikh shrines.*

(bottom) *Two prominent Akali leaders: Jathedar Gurcharan Singh Tohra (to the left), President of the SGPC who has dominated Sikh religious and political activity for several decades; and the late Sant Harchand Singh Longowal.*

MODEL OF SIKH SOCIETY

In the last phase of his life Guru Nanak settled in a small village on the banks of the River Ravi (known as Dera Baba Nanak on the border with Pakistan). Calling the village Kartarpur, God's Abode, he worked there in the fields and shared his produce with others. A community of disciples grew up at Kartarpur but it was a fellowship of ordinary men and women engaged in normal occupations rather than a monastic order. The Guru and his followers would get up before dawn and after ablutions pray together and eat from the community kitchen before attending to the day's work. In the evening they would assemble again for prayers and food, and before going to bed recite *Kirtan Sohila*, hymns of praise. Kartarpur provided a model of living which was to become the basis for the development of Sikh society and the Sikh value system.

DEVELOPMENT OF SIKHISM

Guru Nanak was followed by nine gurus who themselves made significant contributions in evolving institutions for the Sikh community. The second Guru, Angad Dev, developed a distinct script called *Gurmukhi* (from the mouth of the Guru) which became the sole medium for sacred writings. It is in this script that the *Guru Granth*, the holy book of the Sikhs, is written. The third Guru, Amar Dass, strengthened the Sikh movement by instituting *manjis* (literally, string cots) and *piris* (string seats), posts held by important male and female Sikh missionaries in their respective areas. To obliterate the caste distinctions which were the plague of Indian society, the Guru made it obligatory for all visitors to eat in the community kitchen before they could see him. Sikh lore narrates that the contemporary Mughal emperor Akbar who went to see the Guru at Goindwal had to eat *langar* while sitting in line on the floor along with his nobles and servants. Impressed by the Guru's strict practice of equality, Akbar donated the village around which the city of Amritsar was later to grow.

CREATION OF THE KHALSA

Guru Gobind Singh, the tenth and last of the Sikh gurus, was the creator of the Khalsa order. On Baisakhi day in 1699, the Guru called an assembly of the Sikhs at Anandpur (in Punjab). While addressing a packed audience the Guru demanded the heads of five Sikhs. The five who offered themselves and were subsequently initiated into the new order are popularly remembered in Sikh prayers as *Panj Piaras*, the Five Beloved Ones. These five came from different areas and from different castes, three of them from the so-called low castes. Renamed Singh—lion—they were the first followers of Sikhism to adopt its five distinctive symbols: unshorn hair, a comb, short breeches, a steel bracelet and a sword.

SIKH WORSHIP

In contrast to the prevalent Hindu practice of worshipping idols, Sikh gurus advocated worship of the Akal, 'the Timeless One'. The Sikh temple, called *gurdwara*, is not merely a place of worship; it also serves as a refuge for the homeless, the helpless and the destitute. Sikh places of worship are marked by the *Nishan Sahib*, a large yellow triangular flag with the Sikh symbol of *Khanda*. All visitors to these places, irrespective of religious affiliation, are given shelter and served food provided they remove their shoes, wash their feet and cover their heads. No special place within is set aside for important persons; only the *Guru Granth* or Holy Book is given eminence in the centre of the *gurdwara*. There are *gurdwaras* wherever Sikhs live as a community, but some of them in India are deemed historic because of their association with the gurus.

THE GOLDEN TEMPLE

While there are over two hundred such historic shrines, the Golden Temple at Amritsar has been the spiritual and temporal centre of the Sikh world from its inception in 1589. The precise origin of the place where the temple stands today continues to be a subject of controversy among scholars. According to one version, the place traces its origin to pre-historic times. It is believed that a sacred pool, a reservoir (*sar*) of nectar (*amrit*), existed at the place where the fourth Guru, Ram Dass, founded the holy city. According to the *Ramayana*, a popular Hindu epic, Iksvak, a Kshatriya (warrior) king and a predecessor of Lord Rama, performed sacrificial rituals at this place. It is also believed that Lord Rama's consort Sita stayed at Ram Tirath in the vicinity of Amritsar during her exile and gave birth to two sons, Lava and Kusha. Later, in a battle the sons fought with their father, the latter was wounded at the site where the *Dukh Bhanjani Beri* or Sorrow-Despatching Tree now stands. When the identity of the dying Rama was disclosed to Lava and Kusha, they brought *amrit* from the pool and revived their father. The rest of the nectar was immersed in a nearby pond, which from that moment became a famous centre of healing.

This site regained its significance during the period of the Sikh gurus. It was beside this pool that a herb was found which cured a skin disease of the second Guru, Angad Dev. Another popular belief relating to the restorative properties of this *amrit-sar* mentions Rajni, the daughter of Rai Duni Chand, who caused her leper husband to be healed by a dip in the water. Sikh chronicles record that Guru Ram Dass heard about the medicinal efficacy of this pool and decided to convert it into a place of pilgrimage.

FOUNDATION OF THE CITY

There are several versions of the establishment of the new town, the holy tank and the Temple at Amritsar. According to popular accounts, the land on which the fourth Guru established the town, then known as Chak Ram Dass, was donated by the contemporary Mughal ruler Akbar to Bibi Bhani, the daughter of the third Guru, Amar Dass, and wife of the fourth Guru, Ram Dass. It is believed that the Emperor, who halted there on his return from Rajasthan, was so impressed by the third Guru's works of community welfare and especially the institution of *langar*, that he offered the Guru a *jagir* (piece of land) as was the common practice in those days. When the Guru refused the Emperor's gift, Akbar left the title deed as an offering to the free community kitchen. According to another version, Guru Ram Dass purchased this piece of land on a payment of Rs 700 to the *zamindars* (landowners) of Tung village in the then district of Jhabal.

The establishment of Amritsar was an important step in the evolution of the Sikh community. It provided the Sikhs with a spiritual centre and laid the foundations of a commercial centre as well: the encouragement provided by the Guru brought traders, artisans, bankers and other professionals to settle in the newly established township. Because of its location on the main highway, Amritsar soon developed into a hub of commerce and trade in north India.

(top) *The two-storeyed temple is surmounted by a dome completely plated with gold donated by Maharaja Ranjit Singh. After the dome was refurbished, the Harmandir came to be known as Swaran-Mandir or the Golden Temple.*

(bottom) *A model of the Akal Takhat, the seat of Sikh temporal power, is itself a focus of devotion. In the background the main dome of the Akal Takhat is seen under reconstruction.*

Five minutes' walk from the Golden Temple is the Jallianwala Bagh memorial which commemorates the indiscriminate killing of over 300 innocent people under the ordersf Brigadier-General R E H Dyer on 13 April 1919 during the Baisakhi or Spring festival.

CONSTRUCTION OF THE TEMPLE

It was during the period of the fifth Guru, Arjan Dev (1581–1606), that the foundation of the Golden Temple was laid. After consulting Baba Budha, a Sikh saint, Guru Arjan designed the Golden Temple and started its construction. It was built at ground level rather than on a high plinth, in keeping with the Sikh spirit of humility. The temple in the centre of the pool has four doors, signifying that it is open to all the four *Varnas* (castes) into which Indian society was then divided. A causeway links the main entrance, the Darshani Deohri, with the temple. Reflecting the Sikh tradition of religious tolerance, the foundation stone of the Golden Temple was laid by a Muslim divine, Mian Mir. The work of construction was mainly done by the followers of the Guru who contributed their labour voluntarily. And as the news of the completion of the holy tank and the construction of the temple reached the devout, contributions for the project started pouring in. When the temple was almost built the Guru composed the following hymn of thanksgiving:

> *The Creator, the Lord Himself, became my support,*
> *And so no harm came to me.*
> *The Guru hath perfected my Ablution*
> *And, contemplating the Lord, my sins have been washed away.*
> *O Saints, beauteous is the tank of Ram Dass . . .*
> *. . . He who bathes in this tank of the Saints*
> *Receiveth the Supreme Bliss.*

COMPILATION OF THE SIKH SCRIPTURE

To meet the spiritual needs of the Sikhs, Guru Arjan collected the hymns of Guru Nanak and of other gurus along with those of Hindu and Muslim saints, into the *Guru Granth*. Enemies of the Guru, seeking to stir up mischief, complained to the Mughal emperor Akbar that some hymns contained remarks derogatory to the Muslim prophet. The Emperor asked the Guru to show him the holy book under preparation, which the Guru happily did. The following hymn, which was read as God's own word for the occasion, speaks of the catholicity of the message of the *Guru Granth*:

> *One man invokes Ram, another Khuda;*
> *One worships Gosain, another Allah;*
> *Some speak of the Cause of causes,*
> *Others of the Benevolent;*
> *Some talk of the Extender of mercy,*
> *Others of the Merciful;*
> *Some bathe at the Hindu sacred places,*
> *Others visit Mecca; . . .*
> *. . . But he who recognises God's Will, says Nanak,*
> *Knows the secret of the Lord.*

The Emperor, an advocate of universality himself, was touched, and not only paid his obeisance to the work but readily remitted the annual revenue of the *zamindari* of that area as a token of his appreciation. The incident greatly added to the popularity of the new faith among the peasantry who embraced Sikhism in large numbers.

The newly compiled holy book was at first called *Adi Granth*, the Original Book and later became the *Guru Granth*, after the tenth and last Guru declared it to be the ultimate preceptor, the Guru-eternal for the Sikhs. It is large in extent, running into 1432 pages with nearly 7000 hymns, compositions of the first five gurus and 15 saints of different faiths and castes including Shaikh Farid, a Muslim *Sufi*, Ravidas, a shoe-maker, and Sain, a barber. The first copy of the scripture prepared under the care of Guru Arjan was taken to Lahore for binding and brought back with due ceremony to be installed in the Golden Temple in August 1604. Baba Budha, whose devotion to the Guru's house was by then well acknowledged, was appointed the first priest. Except for the periods when the Golden Temple was either forcibly occupied by the enemies of the Sikh Panth or demolished, the *Guru Granth* has always remained in the temple during the day and ceremoniously secluded at night. This routine started by Guru Arjan Dev continues to be the standard practice in the Golden Temple today.

The founding of the holy tank and the Golden Temple in Amritsar along with the installation of *Guru Granth* were two concrete steps towards the crystallisation of the Sikh faith: the former provided a central place of worship, the latter inspiration and guidance to the community. Both have been of great significance in moulding Sikh consciousness. The *Guru Granth* became the permanent repository of the gurus' message, the revealer of the Divine Truth, and the spiritual and religious guide of the Sikhs for all time. It became the source of their literary tradition and shaped their intellectual and cultural environment. It gave form and meaning to their religious style and social customs. When Guru Gobind Singh ended personal guruship and passed on the succession to the *Guru Granth* in perpetuity, it acquired the status of the Guru, and has since been revered as the 'body visible' of the gurus. As such, its role in guaranteeing the integration and permanence of the community and in determining the course of Sikh history has been of prime significance.

CONFLICT WITH THE RULERS

The popularity of the Golden Temple and its founder, Guru Arjan Dev, greatly alarmed the contemporary Mughal emperor, Jahangir. Accusing the Guru of creating an 'empire within the empire' and shielding his rebel son, Khusro, the Emperor ordered the execution of the Guru through torture. Guru Arjan Dev thus became, in May 1606, the first martyr in Sikh history. This caused a setback to the activities and development of Amritsar. But the Guru's son and successor, Guru Hargobind, not only restored the glory of the Golden Temple but also provided a new dimension to Sikh consciousness by wearing two swords—one symbolising *Piri*, sanctity, and the other *Miri*, political authority—thus introducing to Sikhdom the concept of religion-based politics.

THE AKAL TAKHAT

In 1606 Guru Hargobind built the Akal Takhat adjacent to the main entrance of the Golden Temple and declared this to be the seat of the Sikhs' temporal authority. It was here that all political matters concerning the Sikh community were discussed. Since then the chief of the Akal Takhat has exercised the authority to direct the Sikhs on religio-political issues. During the seventh invasion of Ahmad Shah Abdali, the Akal Takhat and the Golden Temple were levelled to the ground, but they were rebuilt by the Sikh chieftains soon afterwards. The collective assembly of the Sikh chiefs also decided to prepare a seal of the Akal Takhat which was to be affixed on various *hukamnamas*, directives issued from time to time. During Maharaja Ranjit Singh's rule (1799–1838), the Akal Takhat was beautified and four more storeys added to the first storey which had been put up in 1774. The golden tower crowning the Akal Takhat was erected under the supervision of Hari Singh Nalwa, who also made a generous donation for the gold-plating.

MANAGEMENT OF THE GOLDEN TEMPLE

Initially Guru Arjan personally oversaw the day-to-day administration and spiritual routines of the Golden Temple, with the assistance of devout Sikhs like Baba Budha and others. Later, the management came under the control of a nephew of the Guru. The tenth Guru, Gobind Singh, in 1721 appointed Bhai Mani Singh, a devout and scholarly Sikh, to head the Golden Temple, and he brought about major improvements in its management. But the emerging Sikh movement was seen as a threat by the contemporary rulers, who sent a strong military contingent to besiege the temple complex and to punish the devotees gathered there. For the first time a police post was set up near the temple and a military detachment under Aslam Khan, the governor of Lahore, was sent to suppress the Sikhs. But under the guidance of Bhai Mani Singh the Sikhs put up a strong defence and repelled the enemy. Later, stronger and bigger contingents were sent to suppress them. The retribution threatened their very existence. They were declared outlaws, prices were put on their heads and those giving them protection faced disastrous consequences. During this period of persecution, Banda Singh Bahadur, the brave leader of the Sikh community after Guru Gobind Singh's death, was caught, taken to Delhi in a cage and put to death along with a large number of his followers.

MUGHAL ATTACK ON THE GOLDEN TEMPLE

Persecution at the hands of the rulers forced many Sikhs to leave their homes and seek shelter in the hills. While many of the Sikhs serving at the Golden Temple left for safer places, Bhai Mani Singh remained at his post, helping to resolve the differences between the two factions into which the Sikhs had divided after Guru Gobind Singh's death. When he thought that political conditions were a little more favourable, Mani Singh decided to celebrate the Baisakhi and Diwali festivals at the temple. These had remained suspended for many years because of the hostile attitude of the state. After securing permission from Zakariya Khan, the Governor of Lahore, against payment of *jazia* (capitation tax), Mani Singh invited the Sikhs to come out of their hideouts to celebrate Baisakhi. But those who gathered for the celebration were betrayed and the temple was besieged by the Mughal forces. Mani Singh and his companions were arrested and taken to Lahore, where they were put to death. The temple was occupied by the invaders, and the sacred tank filled with debris. It was a Sikh hero, Jassa Singh Ahluwalia, who liberated the temple in March 1748. That year the Baisakhi festival was celebrated in the Golden Temple by the Sikhs with great enthusiasm.

GOLD-PLATING OF THE TEMPLE

When the Mughal hold began weakening at the centre, the Sikhs in the north and Marathas in the west organised themselves into guerilla bands and, after defeating the local deputies of the Mughal rulers, set up independent principalities. In Punjab, Ranjit Singh founded an empire which he ruled as Maharaja for nearly 40 years (1799–1838). It was during his rule that the temple was covered with gold-plated copper sheets and hence came to be called *Swaran-Mandir*—the Golden Temple. A gold plate at the main entrance of the central shrine records that 'the Guru was kind enough to allow the privilege of service to the temple to his humble servant Ranjit Singh'.

ART AND ARCHITECTURE OF THE GOLDEN TEMPLE

The Golden Temple was redecorated by master craftsmen under Ranjit Singh's instructions, and he himself took a keen interest in the details of the work. The stone inlay and floral decoration was executed by expert Muslim artisans, and the murals by painters from the famous Kangra school of art. In terms of its architectural style, the Golden Temple stands out as unique among all the shrines of India. In the words of the art critic K.S. Kang, 'The main structure rises from the centre of the sacred pool, 150 metres square, approached by a causeway about 60 metres long. An archway on the western side of the pool opens on to the causeway, bordered with balustrades of fretted marble, and, at close intervals, there are standard lamps, their great lanterns set upon marble columns. The 52-metre square-based Hari-Mandir, to which the causeway leads, stands on a 20-metre square platform. Its lower parts are of white marble, but the upper parts are covered with plates of gilded copper.'

In the interior, on the ground floor, is the *Guru Granth*, placed under a decorated canopy studded with jewels. On the first floor is the *Shish Mahal* or Hall of Mirrors; it has a square central opening over the ground floor, with a narrow circumambulatory passage around the opening. Its ceiling is inlaid with small pieces of reflecting glass of various sizes and shapes, and its walls are richly embellished with designs, mostly floral in character. Above the *Shish Mahal* is a small square pavilion, surmounted by a low fluted golden dome, and lined at its base with a number of smaller domes. The walls of the two lower storeys, forming parapets, terminate with several rounded pinnacles. There are four *chhatris* or kiosks at the corners. The combination of dozens of large, medium and miniature domes of gilded copper creates a dazzling effect, enhanced by the reflection in the water below.

The construction of a number of *bungas* provided accommodation for pilgrims to the Golden Temple. As a token of his gratitude to the Guru, Ranjit Singh used to make large offerings to the temple whenever he visited Amritsar or when he achieved success on his various military campaigns. According to popular accounts, valuables presented to Ranjit Singh by other rulers or visitors were offered by him in turn to the Golden Temple. In the *toshakhana* (treasure house) of the Golden Temple there were many precious articles such as a canopy embedded with about 20 pounds of gold and studded with diamonds, emeralds, rubies and pearls; a bejewelled armband worth millions of rupees; another equally precious canopy; a sword with a gold handle studded with jewels and pearls; two golden portals with floral designs and other valuables presented by Maharaja Ranjit Singh. Three walls of the Hari-Mandir were inlaid with gold provided by the Maharaja, and much of the white marble, too, was contributed by him. The best

The interior of the Golden Temple is lavishly decorated with carved marble work together with painted and gilded designs.

(top) *Kneeling in homage at the entrance of the temple.*

(bottom) *The* langar *or community kitchen serves food throughout the day and night to all visitors, irrespective of their caste or creed.*

artists available were employed for the stone inlay work. For this 'service' in gold and marble, the Maharaja contributed over 16 lakh rupees, amounting to a quarter of the total estimated cost.

While the management of the Golden Temple during the rule of Ranjit Singh was in the hands of Bhai Sant Singh and other prominent Sikhs, the Akalis—zealous guardians of the Akal Takhat and other religious places—started exercising considerable influence in matters concerning Sikh ethics. Akali Phula Singh, who was appointed chief of the Akal Takhat, enjoyed so much moral authority that he could reprimand even the Maharaja for moral lapses on his part. We are told that when Ranjit Singh married a beautiful Muslim courtesan named Moran he was summoned to the Akal Takhat by Akali Phula Singh, tied to a tree and ordered to undergo public flogging for having dared to violate the Sikh canon.

GOLDEN TEMPLE UNDER BRITISH CONTROL

After the death of Ranjit Singh in 1838 and the defeat of the Sikh forces in the two Anglo-Sikh wars, the Sikh kingdom was annexed by the British Empire in 1849. Realising the importance of the Golden Temple and other Sikh shrines, the British government contrived to control them by proxy, and by this means initially to win over the Sikhs and later, during the Indian independence movement, to attack the forces of nationalism. Priests of the Akal Takhat, backed by the British imperial regime, actually issued a *hukamnama* against Sikh supporters of the nationalist struggle and later honoured General Dyer (who ordered the Jallianwala Bagh massacre at Amritsar in 1919) with a *saropa* (robe of honour).

While the tragedy of Jallianwala lent an impetus to the struggle for independence from British imperial rule, the treacherous and sacrilegious actions of the government-appointed priests of the Golden Temple brought home to the Sikhs the need to free their *gurdwaras* from official control as early as possible.

GURDWARA REFORM MOVEMENT

With the general awakening among the Sikhs in the early decades of the 20th century, the urge to reform grew. Sikh reformers started organising public meetings against the government-appointed manager of the Golden Temple and brought about his resignation in 1920. In another initiative the *Khalsa Biradari* of Amritsar led a procession of some of the so-called low castes into the Golden Temple; the priests had earlier debarred them from entry except at prescribed hours. The mass action had a salutary effect. The priests fled, the reforming party took over and conducted the religious duties on a voluntary basis, and a Provisional Committee for the management of the Golden Temple was appointed.

Popular control over the Golden Temple greatly strengthened the movement for *gurdwara* reform and set the stage for the Akali struggle to repossess Sikh shrines. During their five years' struggle (1920–1925), the reformers succeeded in dislodging the government-supported *mahants* and priests from their hereditary control of the shrines and restoring the tradition of democratic management in the *gurdwaras*. Two powerful bodies, the Shiromani Akali Dal and the Shiromani Gurdwara Parbandhak Committee (SGPC), were formed. The Golden Temple and the Akal Takhat became major centres of Sikh activity and attracted worldwide attention. National leaders like Mahatma Gandhi, Jawaharlal Nehru, Maulana Shaukat Ali, Dr Kitchlew and Lala Lajpat Rai visited the Golden Temple, Nankana Sahib and Gangsar Jaito to express their solidarity with the Sikh reformers.

Having failed to isolate the Akali reformers, the British rulers tried to suppress the struggle through police action. In the Akali struggle at Guru-ka-Bagh, more than 6000 Akali volunteers were imprisoned, nearly 1500 suffered injuries and many were killed. During another phase of *gurdwara* reform, the British police opened fire at a group of 500 Akalis who were trying to resume the interrupted *akhand path* at Gurdwara Gangsar Jaito. The movement of *gurdwara* reform impressed Jawaharlal Nehru, who, during a spell of imprisonment in Nabha, one of the princely Sikh states, observed the movement for himself and became a great admirer of the peaceful Akali struggle. In return for large-scale suffering and sacrifice, the Akali movement secured for the Sikhs, in the form of the Sikh Gurdwaras and Shrines Act of 1925, undisputed and exclusive control over the historic shrines. The movement also won for Sikhs a system of *gurdwara* elections which was, and continues to be, a unique feature; no other social or religious group anywhere in the world seems to exercise similar constitutional rights.

Traditional motifs of auspicious floral designs are used to adorn the interiors.

KAR SEWA IN THE GOLDEN TEMPLE

The enthusiasm generated among the Sikh masses by the movement for *gurdwara* reform found expression in the historic Kar Sewa of 1923. The newly formed SGPC prepared a plan for the long-due desilting of the holy tank. Cleaning started on 17 June, by specially chosen *Panj Piaras*, who inaugurated the work with gold spades and silver baskets after performing prayer and other religious ceremonies—the tools still grace the treasury (*toshakhana*) in Amritsar. Thousands of Sikhs from all over India and abroad came to participate in the project. A large number of Hindu and Muslim devotees of the Sikh gurus also joined their Sikh brethren in volunteering their labour.

Great emphasis is laid on the Sikh tradition of early rising, bathing and meditation. That is why when one visits the Golden Temple even before sunrise, one sees devotees listening to devotional music after a dip in the sacred tank. On Amavas and other festive days large crowds of pilgrims visit the temple and bathe in the tank. There are special celebrations on occasions such as the birthday of Guru Ram Dass, the founder of the city, as well as Diwali and Guru Nanak's birth anniversary, when the temple complex is illuminated and fireworks displays are held. On such occasions the valuables in the treasury are also displayed.

ADJOINING BUILDINGS

Adjacent to the Golden Temple is a spacious hall where *langar* is prepared and served by the devotees to the visitors and the needy. This is one of the Sikh institutions in which the gurus' teachings of equality among human beings are practised every day.

Service forms an essential part of the Sikh credo; thus, apart from cooking and serving meals in the free kitchen, the Sikhs also help the poor and needy through free medical aid. The temple complex has a free hospital, the Guru Ram Dass Hospital, with a highly qualified staff. To accommodate visitors from outside, the Guru Ram Dass Sarai offers devotees, and others in need, free board and lodging. Recently two new buildings, Guru Nanak Niwas and Akal Rest House, have been added to the residential complex to meet the requirements of pilgrims. Adjacent to the Sarai is the Teja Singh Samundri Hall which houses the SGPC and the administrative staff. The Golden Temple complex had a rich Sikh reference library which was destroyed during the Operation Blue Star in 1984. On the first

(above) *Popular calendar or poster art often depicts the ten gurus with a central portrait of Guru Nanak*

floor of the main entrance to the Golden Temple complex is the Central Sikh Museum displaying rare paintings on themes relating to Sikh history. The museum also has a rich collection of coins, old documents, *hukamnamas*, rare manuscripts and arms.

GOLDEN TEMPLE AND POPULAR MOVEMENTS

The Golden Temple and the Akal Takhat have long been established as the hub of Sikh religio-political activities. It was from the Akal Takhat that important *hukamnamas* were issued, first by the Sikh gurus and later by the *Jathedars* of the Takhat, which are considered binding on all followers of the Sikh faith wherever they live. Not even a powerful monarch like Ranjit Singh dared to defy the authority of the Akal Takhat. When Sikh chieftains had to settle mutual problems or evolve a consensus on some major issues affecting the destiny of the community, they invariably met at the Akal Takhat and resolved their differences through *gurmata*, a resolution passed by the assembly of Sikhs. During the British rule in the Punjab, the Golden Temple and the Akal Takhat were quite often used to promote imperial interests until the Akali movement made them the hub of Akali and nationalist struggle. It was from the Golden Temple complex that the Akali leadership conducted its propaganda and issued daily communiqués explaining its position on different issues. After the partition of India, it was from the Akal Takhat that the Shiromani Akali Dal launched its powerful struggle for the creation of Punjabi Suba. During ten years of agitation the Golden Temple complex remained the centre of Akali activities and the focus of attention for the world media.

In the last two decades the Golden Temple complex has been the arena of conflict between the Akali leadership and the government at the centre. Various agitations against the government have been launched from the temple complex. Notwithstanding the turmoil of political strife in the Punjab in recent years, the devout continue to throng the Golden Temple, which remains a source of spiritual inspiration to all who seek God.

(right) *Miniature replicas of the Golden Temple are often presented to important visitors.*

S. Tejwant Singh   Dalai Lama

(opposite page) *Devotees enter through the Darshani Deohri and proceed along the elegant 60-metre causeway leading to the Harmandir Sahib.*

During Diwali, the festival of lights celebrated throughout India in October-November, the Golden Temple is decorated. Devotees light lamps and candles around the sarovar while fireworks illuminate the night sky.

In 1860 William Simpson painted a scene of the courtyard of the temple and the Akal Takhat. Built by the sixth Guru, Hargobind, the Akal Takhat or Throne of the Almighty is the seat of Sikh temporal authority and is where elected council members meet to debate on religio-political matters.

The Golden Temple is surrounded by an open paved passageway with four ornamental gates facing the cardinal directions. The other structures that dominate the skyline are the bungas or towers beside which are hostels for pilgrims.

Detail of the upper storey of the Golden Temple.

At the Akal Takhat religious songs or kirtan are sung by members of the community as part of daily worship. Women freely participate in the rituals of the Sikh faith.

(above) *Details of the golden panels covering the temple incorporate designs inherited from both the Hindu and Islamic traditions.*

(left) *The hybrid Islamic dome over the sanctum of the temple is surmounted by Hindu motifs such as the symbolic pot (kalash) of* amrit, *nectar of immortality, set within a lotus petal base.*

(opposite page) *Around the temple is a paved passageway called the* parikrama *for the ritual circumambulation of the shrine. Each panel of the elaborate marble mosaic work of the* parikrama *differs from the next in design. The mosaic is created out of coloured marble cut in various shapes and embedded in the ground.*

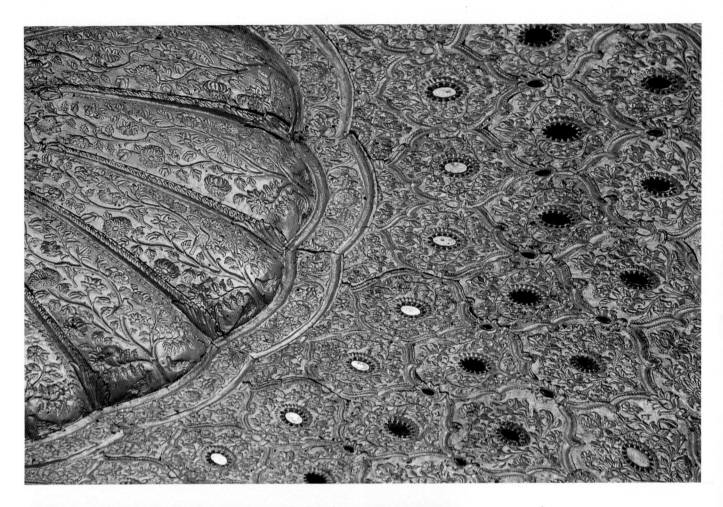

The interiors are elaborately adorned with painted murals, stucco work and gilded mirror-work patterns. The floral motifs derived from nature are symbols of rejuvenation, continuity, abundance and prosperity.

(following pages) Tranquillity and serene calm permeates the atmosphere of the temple at dawn and dusk.

(far left) *The golden plaque above the entrance which commemorates the service rendered to the temple by Maharaja Ranjit Singh.*

(opposite page) *The Golden Temple appears like an exquisite casket of gold floating in the peaceful Waters of Immortality.*

(above) *A pious discipline pervades the crowds as worshippers gather to pay homage at the Harmandir Sahib. Some carry large plates of sweets or prasad to offer to the temple. This is blessed and a little is returned so that the devotees can eat of the consecrated food.*

(left) *Drawing nearer to the temple, visitors are able to see the intricate and ornate decorations standing out on the relatively simple architectural structure of the shrine.*

*Saffron yellow, the colour once worn by martyrs
and religious heroes, is associated with sacrifice
and honour. This vibrant colour dominates the
temple surroundings and is worn by young and old
to reaffirm their faith and pledge to duty.*

(top) *Shahidi Khuh, the Martyr's
Well where villagers took
refuge during the massacre
instigated by General Dyer
in 1919.*

(above) *Rituals at the temple are reminiscent of a martial past with the blowing of a traditional wind instrument like a horn that announces the commencement of prayer.*

(opposite page) *The glimmering jewel-like temple framed by its pure white arched entrance.*

Lighting of lamps for Diwali festival is symbolic of the removal of darkness and ignorance. Pure limitless light, the grace of the Almighty, says the Sikh prayer, exists in all human beings.

*Faithful devotees sip the Water of Immortality.
According to Sikh tradition, Bhai Kanahiya, a
follower of Guru Gobind Singh, served water to
the injured and also to the fallen soldiers of the
enemy. This act is understood as an example
of true Sikh altruism and egalitarian service.
Devotees consider it an honourable privilege
to serve water to all who visit the temple.*

Collective and individual prayer at the temple.

(opposite page)
(top left) *Religious processions feature as part of the celebrations of the birthday of Guru Nanak and other festive occasions. Local school-children participate in these festivities.*

(bottom left) *A young couple taking blessings after their wedding.*

The imposing gateways of the Golden Temple which keep the bustle of the outside world away and protect the sanctified peace of the inner courtyard and sanctum.

The temple serves many purposes: a place to offer flowers of thanksgiving for blessings received, to demonstrate and reaffirm one's faith, to meet and share the warmth of human affection, to learn and teach and to make supplications and pray for divine favours.

(above and top right) *The four doors of the temple are open to all directions and faiths.*

(bottom right) *Memorial to Baba Deep Singh, a great Sikh martyr who continued to defend the faith though he was mortally wounded. He fell at this spot on the parikrama of the temple which is honoured with garlands.*

(opposite page)

(top) *Prayers are offered at various sacred points of the* parikrama. *Dukh Bhanjani Beri is an ancient jujube tree that is believed to take away all sorrow and suffering.*

(bottom left) *All offerings made to the temple are utilised to run the community kitchen and other charitable activities.*

(bottom right) *The holy book, the Guru Granth, carried in a golden palanquin.*

There is no image worship in the Sikh gurdwara. The holy book which contains the principal teachings was declared by Guru Gobind, the tenth Guru, as the Guru Granth Sahib or the Guru Eternal for all Sikhs. It is taken out during the ambrosial hour of the dawn in a golden palanquin and installed in the sanctum. Throughout the day passages are read and devotees pay their respects to it. After the evening service the holy book is taken back to the Kotha Sahib or resting place with due ceremony.

(above) *The first coin issued by Maharaja Ranjit Singh, which in accordance to the belief does not carry his insignia but the words 'Akal Sahai', meaning Glory to the Lord.*

(left and right) *Priceless gifts presented by Maharaja Ranjit Singh and other Sikh chiefs are now stored in the toshakhana or treasury above the Darshani Deohri and are displayed only on festive occasions.*

(left) *An inscription recording a miracle that took place on 30 April 1877. A powerful light entered the temple sanctum and disappeared from the gate without causing any damage to the Holy Book and the devotees within.*

(opposite page) *Exuberant childern during a festival.*

To practise social and religious equality the Sikh gurus started the institution of the langer, the free community kitchen. Every Sikh shrine has a kitchen where all visitors, irrespective of their social status or wealth, colour or creed, partake of food prepared by the devotees.

(above) An exemplary painting by Bodh Raj of Akbar, the Mughal Emperor of India sharing a meal with his nobles and servants during his visit to the fourth Guru, Ram Dass.

61

(above) *Temple official on duty.*

(opposite page) *Conspicuous by their head gear, double-edged swords and dark blue and saffron yellow garments, the Nihangs (literally dragons) are members of an order instituted by the tenth Guru. They are also called Akalis (deathless or immortal) and were known for their willingness to sacrifice their lives for the protection of their faith and places of Sikh worship.*

(above) *Pamphlets, souvenirs, swords and the metal bracelet or kara worn by Sikhs, are sold in shops around the temple.*

(left) *Bhagat Puran Singh has become a legend throughout the Punjab for his life-long devotion to the service of the poor and destitute. Moved by the pitiable condition of a young leper in 1934, when he was only ten years old, he resolved to open a leprosy home and his work continues as he finds homes and support for orphans and others.*

(opposite page) *Pilgrims, travellers and visitors to religious fairs and festivals arrive in their own distinctive attire, proudly proclaiming their faith irrespective of age.*

The resplendent interiors of the Golden Temple make a fitting shrine for the Guru Granth. The decoration is carefully preserved and retouched from time to time.

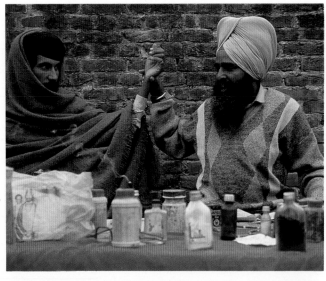

Outside the temple walls the streets are lined with shops selling pictures, posters, flowers and food offerings or prasad. Pilgrims coming from great distances make annual purchases of souvenirs and religious items, while others consult their teachers and doctors.

As a result of royal patronage a hybrid style of art evolved in the Punjab absorbing features from Hindu and Muslim architecture. The central dome of the Harmandir Sahib is complemented by smaller domes rising out of stylised lotus petals. The author of the gilt work is said to be a goldsmith, Harnam Dass, from Amritsar.

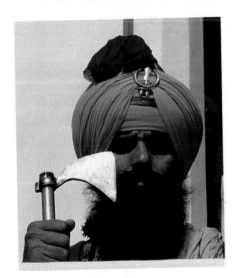

The turban is worn with great pride and dignity by the male member of the Sikh community in accordance with the religious code. Throughout Punjab, a great variety of styles and techniques of tying the turban can be seen.

Beyond the temple life goes on. Punjab, the land of the five major rivers, is often described as the 'granary and bread basket of India', and Punjabis are known for their hard work and enterprise. Although agriculture in the Punjab has been modernised in recent years, life on the farm is still backbreaking. The younger generation, however, now enjoy the privilege of schooling.

Guru Gobind Singh encouraged the order of the Nihangs to practise martial arts so that they may serve and protect the holy shrines. Horse-riding, archery and sword fighting are some of the skills perfected by this order. Every year on the Hola Mohala festival in Anantpur (Punjab) various groups of Nihangs display their traditional arts.

AKAL TAKHAT, literally the 'Throne of the Almighty', was built by the sixth Guru Hargobind in 1606, in the precincts of the Golden Temple as the central seat of the Sikh temporal authority. All important decisions concerning the political destiny of the Sikh community have invariably been taken from the Takhat. The Akal Takhat is one of the five seats of authority in the Sikh faith, the others being Takhat Sri Patna Sahib, Hazoor Sahib, Kesgarh Sahib and Damdama Sahib. During the army action in 1984 the Akal Takhat was badly damaged and was subsequently repaired through officially sponsored agencies. The militant Sikh leadership did not approve of this and after demolishing the whole structure, raised a new building through Kar Sewa.

AKALI, literally 'immortal', was first used by Guru Gobind Singh for those of his followers who were prepared to sacrifice everything for the protection of their religious places. Their dark blue garments, typical head-dress (a tall conical turban festooned with quoits), double-edged swords and *kirpan* (small swords) and their fanatical temperament made them zealous fighters for religious causes. The Akalis were known for their purity of character and sincerity of conviction and commanded great respect in the Sikh community. In the field of religion they enjoyed a unique position and were regarded as the guardians of the Akal Takhat at Amritsar and other important *gurdwaras*. During the dark days of Sikh history (1708–1799) they had to undergo great hardship in keeping alive the torch of Sikhism. But during Maharaja Ranjit Singh's rule and some time after most of them retired to an easy life and lost much of their old spir-

it. In the *gurdwara* reform movement of 1920–1925 the Akalis played a significant role in India's struggle for freedom. These days the epithet of 'Akali' is used for those who are members of political organisations called Akali Dals.

AKHAND PATH is an uninterrupted reading of the *Guru Granth* from beginning to end, undertaken by a series of readers to ensure that no break occurs. It takes about 48 hours and is expected to be conducted with a certain solemnity: the words are to be read accurately and pronounced clearly, so that all listeners can easily hear and understand. In some major *gurdwaras* a chain of *akhand paths* is a permanent feature of worship, a new one beginning as the last one ends. Normally they take place at *gurpurabs*, ending before dawn on the day of the celebration. Families arrange *akhand paths* on occasions such as weddings, death anniversaries, and moving into a new house or new business premises. The reading is ended with a formal ceremony, known as *bhog*.

The origin of the *akhand path* is uncertain but it can possibly be traced to the 18th century. In those turbulent times it was a means of spiritually uniting and strengthening scattered and threatened groups. Its popularity increased with the availability of printed copies of the *Guru Granth* in the 19th century.

AMRIT, literally nectar, is associated with the Sikh baptismal ritual. It is made from water into which sugar crystals are stirred with a double-edged sword called *khanda* to the accompaniment of scriptural recitation, and administered to Sikhs at their formal initiation into the order of the Khalsa. Guru Gobind Singh performed the first baptism while creating the order of the Khalsa on the

Baisakhi of 1699 at Gurdwara Kesgarh Sahib in Anandpur Sahib. The *amrit* ceremony is also performed at other religious places on important days.

BAISAKHI, the (spring) harvest festival of Punjab, heralds the new year according to the Sikh calendar. The festival generally falls on the 13th of April every year with rare exceptions. From the time of the third Guru, Amar Das, the Sikhs have assembled in the presence of the Guru on Baisakhi. It was also on the Baisakhi of 1699 that the tenth Guru, Gobind Singh, created the order of the Khalsa.

GHALUGHARA, meaning massacre, is used for two major tragic events of Sikh history known as the smaller and bigger holocausts—the first in 1746, in which nearly 7000 Sikhs were killed near Lahore, and the second in 1762, when about 25,000 people, including women and children, were massacred.

GURMATA, literally 'Guru's resolution', is generally a decision arrived at through consensus, either at the Akal Takhat or in any other *gurdwara*. Such a resolution, generally taken on vital issues concerning the Sikh community, is considered binding on all Sikhs. A *gurmata* is generally passed by a collective assembly of the Sikh community after prior public announcement and after inviting all important representatives. Traditionally, important *gurmatas* were passed during the festivals of Hola Mohalla, Baisakhi and Diwali; all *gurmatas* are passed in the presence of the *Guru Granth*.

HUKAMNAMA, literally 'royal command', refers to the injunctions issued by the Sikh gurus, by Banda Bahadur and subsequently by the *jathedars* of the five Takhats. The *hukamnama* is considered to be a command of the gurus and, therefore, binding on all.

JATHA refers to a band of volunteers or devotees going on pilgrimage. This word is also used for sub-groups within Sikhism and for Akali volunteers who played a vital role in liberating the shrines from the control of hereditary managers. The associated term *Jathedar* refers to the leader of such a group. Originally the term was used for leaders of Sikh volunteers who devoted themselves to full-time voluntary service of the *Panth*. During the Akali Movement for Reform in Sikh Shrines the *Jathas* and *Jathedars* came into prominence because of their non-violent victorious struggle against the British which resulted in the liberation of the Sikh shrines from the hereditary control of the *mahants*.

KAR SEWA, work performed through voluntary labour, is used in the Sikh context mainly for the purpose of building Sikh temples and cleaning holy tanks. It is also used for the removal of silt every 50 years from the sacred tank of the Golden Temple. The first such important *Kar Sewa* had been undertaken during the 1923 Gurdwara Reform Movement. In 1973 another *Kar Sewa* was performed according to the schedule. A special *Kar Sewa* was performed in 1985 because of the desecration of the sacred tank during the 1984 army operation in the Golden Temple complex.

KHALSA is used for the order of baptised Sikhs founded by Guru Gobind Singh on the Baisakhi of 1699. The word means 'pure' but in the present context it means 'God's own', or 'God-oriented people'. Guru Gobind Singh gave the Khalsa distinguishing marks known as the Five K's and a code of conduct which gave the members of the new order a distinct spiritual and physical identity. The Five K's enjoined upon all the baptised Sikhs are *Kesh* (untrimmed hair), *Kangha* (a wooden comb), *Kara* (an iron bracelet), *Kacha* (a pair of drawers) and *Kirpan* (a small sword). These symbols were prescribed by the tenth Guru to provide an identity to the disparate members of the newly created order.

LANGAR is the serving of free meals in the community kitchen of a Sikh temple. The institution of *langar* was started by Guru Nanak with the objective of demonstrating equality. The food is prepared by the devout through voluntary labour, and rations are provided either by followers or by the management of the temple. The volunteers prepare the food and also clean utensils, sweep and mop the floors etc.

MAHANTS were hereditary custodians of the Sikh shrines. In the early stages of *gurdwara* management, they enjoyed the confidence and reverence of the followers of the Sikh faith. Later these *mahants* became corrupt and started ignoring the popular will and were removed from their hereditary positions by Sikh reformers.

PANJ PIARAS, meaning the 'Five Beloved Ones', is the term used for five baptised Sikhs who lead important processions. It commemorates Guru Gobind Singh's call for the historic assembly of the Sikhs on Baisakhi 1699 at Anandpur, at which he appeared with an unsheathed sword demanding the head of a Sikh. The audience gazed in awed silence as the Guru twice repeated his call. Bhai Daya Ram of Lahore responded and was taken to a nearby tent. A little later the Guru reappeared, this time his sword dripping

with blood. He demanded another head, and this time Dharam Dass came forward. In response to three more calls Mohkam Chand, Himmat Rai and Sahib Chand also came forward. After some moments of suspense the Guru brought the five Sikhs out of the tent attired in the saffron-coloured new robes of the Khalsa, with neatly tied blue turbans. He introduced them as his *Panj Piaras*, and gave them the title of 'Bhai' as a prefix to their names. Their act of faith is remembered with reverence in the daily Sikh prayers.

SANGAT means a congregation of believers, especially in a *gurdwara*. The Sikh religion attaches great importance to this concept and the followers of the faith are enjoined to assemble in *sangat* every morning and evening to listen to the recitations of the *Guru Granth* and to devotional music. The importance of the concept of *sangat* is evident from the fact that on major issues the decisions of the *sangat* carried precedence over those of the Gurus.

SAROPA is a robe of honour presented by the priest or head priest of a Sikh temple to any one or more members of the community or other dignitaries to whom formal respect or gratitude has to be shown. Generally it is a mustard coloured length of cotton cloth, or a shawl which is draped ceremoniously across the shoulders. According to Sikh tradition the *saropa* is presented to those who have made or are prepared to make great personal sacrifice for a good religious or social cause.

SAT SRI AKAL, the Sikh form of salutation or greeting, literally means 'truth is eternal'. The Sikhs are enjoined to use this as a form of greeting with palms joined together and raised.

The photographer

Sondeep Shankar is the picture editor for the Observer Group of Newspapers. Previously senior photographer for the *Times of India* in Delhi, he has recently photographed an extensive study of the 'Havelis of Old Delhi'. He has also contributed pictures to books on Kashmir, Himachal Pradesh and the Gurudwaras of India.

The author

Dr Mohinder Singh wrote his doctoral thesis on the Akali Movement and has published numerous books on Sikh history. Formerly Director of the Guru Nanak Foundation and Professor of History at Punjab University in Patilia, he is currently Director of the National Institute of Punjab Studies, New Delhi.

GS/61/01